BESIDE YOURSELF, AROUND YOURSELF, AND BACK TO YOURSELF

Maja Spencer

2023

I tried my best to write this book concisely. As I always say, I don't want to "kill" the reader with words. No need for unnecessary words — that is my rule number one. If you have read some of my books, you must have noticed that they differ quite a bit from each other. I have written both non-fiction and fiction; however, all my books have something in common – each is meant to convey a specific message and help someone. This book is no exception. It is meant to be a short, practical guide in which I describe the method I call "the separation method". You may wonder how I came up with it and why I want to share it. It is all very simple – I came up with it after years of education and practical experience. I wish to share it because I have seen it help many people. Perhaps someone else has developed a similar method – that is quite possible. I have never heard anyone talk about it, nor have the psychologists I have met. Therefore, I thought it would be a useful and interesting thing to share.

I will use the term "client" to refer to a person who needs professional help. By "professional," I mean a life coach, psychologist, counselor, psychotherapist, sponsor, or any other experienced individual who helps another person resolve problems in their life.

As you read this book, there are millions of life coaches, counselors, psychologists, and other professionals offering their services. Each of them is doing their job for their own motives – from those primarily motivated by money to those motivated by passion, the need to use their knowledge for something good, and altruism. The latter is the reason this book came into existence. If it helps you help other people, that is sufficient for me. The greatest reward I could ever receive is the notion that someone out there has benefited from my work and learned from my experience. If you knew me, this would make sense; however, you probably don't, so let me make a short introduction. Who on Earth am I, and why should you read this book?

A long time ago, I graduated from the University of Political Sciences, the Department of International Relations (Diplomacy). As future diplomats, we had to learn many things; there were many different courses, such as sociology, philosophy, history (of political theories, economics, political systems, diplomatic history, and much more), economics, language, and culture studies… I kid you not—we even had "cybernetics and management." In all of those, there was a lot of psychology. It was everywhere. To be a good diplomat, to know how to negotiate and reach the optimal outcome, one has to know many things I mentioned, but above all, one must have extensive knowledge of psychology and be good at it in practice. During my university studies, I learned psychology in practice. That experience provided me with invaluable tools that I would be using later in life, pretty much every day, or at least every time I interacted with a human being (and some other animals as well). I have been interested in the humanities since I was a teenager. I completed my university studies when I was twenty-two (as I was living in post-war Serbia, I was in a hurry to start working and earning money. The times were rough for most of us. My father, a lawyer (an honest type of lawyer, a species that is getting dangerously close to extinction), never wanted to defend bad people or war criminals; that took a toll on his income and, subsequently, on our family. I can't blame him for that; I would have done the same. However, it was clear to me that I had to start working to help my family. I lived in Belgrade, away from my family, and I was a loner in a way. I think it was what I needed at the time – peace and quiet, time and space so that I could study and work. I was never a party person… One could easily call me a nerd—but without the stereotypical appearance, which made things harder for me. Even today, people can't tell I am a nerd until they get to know me well. That made things a bit difficult at times; I spent a lot of time explaining to potential employers or future associates that being a young, somewhat attractive woman did not make me less knowledgeable, less competent, less reliable, less hard-working, less loyal, or less disciplined.

When I was around nineteen, my plan was to work for the Serbian Security Information Agency. As I learned more about people, governments, politics, and the people I met, I changed my mind, and I am very glad I did. Still, my interest in the humanities and in human beings hasn't changed; it has only grown. (In the meantime, I have also completed my Master's studies in psychology.)

My finishing thesis at my first university (Political Sciences) was "The Art of Manipulation", and I wrote it with pleasure and ease. "Why manipulation?" you might ask. Let me explain.

Let's start by explaining what manipulation really is. "But I know what it is," you will say. Yes, we all know what the "modern" meaning of the word is. It is a bad word, often related to Niccolo Machiavelli (who, by the way, was not a bad guy at all). In the modern sense, manipulation means taking advantage of something or someone for your own gain. And yes, that happens much more than it should, in some very ugly forms. But does it have to be that way?

Manipulation: *Manus* + *pulare* – handling something, turning it, changing it. Is that a bad thing?

Let's do something fun now. Can you remember all the times (or just one time – it is sufficient) when you talked someone into or out of something, for their own good, and later they even thanked you? Do you remember all the times when you made your kid do something that was good for them, even though they didn't feel like doing it at that moment, or perhaps you talked them into not giving up? Do you remember convincing yourself of something that was necessary to change your mood, help you leave a bad situation, or improve? … And then we get to (are you ready?)... therapy. Therapy is nothing but manipulation. If you prefer, and to avoid confusion (since "manipulation" has become a bad word), I can use the word "influence". What does a therapist do? As a therapist (or a life coach, psychologist, etc.), your job is to literally change someone's mind. To change the way they think and feel. Helping a person, or better said, enabling them to help themselves, certainly depends on your knowledge, but more than that – it depends on your instincts and your talent to – yes, I will say it in a politically correct way – influence a person. After I finished my university studies, I realized that the knowledge I had acquired was useful in many different fields. You need to sell something? No problem. Do you need a security consultant? You need help with PR and propaganda (marketing is a nicer word, but they are the same thing, aren't they ?) You need help resolving conflicts? You need help maintaining or changing any kind of system? No problem. And so I worked with different kinds of people; some of those companies were horrible, and I left quickly; some were even more horrible, but I stayed because I needed a job. But there were two things that always followed me around, like loyal dogs: my knowledge of psychology and my instincts. I only have those to thank for having kept not only my job but also my sanity. Of course, it made me think about all the people who might benefit from these two things. I have always been "flirting" with psychopathology; I have seen so much, and I couldn't help but think: "How can these people be helped? How can these things be prevented? How can these things be resolved?"

And it was only natural to start my own research, which resulted in some of my books. I wrote them in a very clear, concise way; I wanted them to be understandable to an adolescent. I always felt that it was they, the young brains, who were in the deepest trouble and needed attention and some kind of help. I spent more than fifteen years studying violent psychopaths, as well as some other subjects. At one point, I felt it was more important to turn to "regular" people suffering from trauma; there were so many of them, and I believed I could actually change something for them. (As you probably know, you can't do much to change a violent psychopath; all you can do is study them, hoping that someday, society will take your research into consideration and perhaps change certain things. And you know how hard *that* usually is.) This book is very different from my other books. Nevertheless, in all of them, I used every opportunity to share something I found useful with the readers. We are not only "homo sapiens"; we are also *"homo ludens"*. We don't only think; we like to play games, and we are fun-loving animals. If something is fun, we tend to become quickly interested in it and learn faster. (As you know, children learn best through playing—unlike dogs, for example, who learn best through reward. However, it sometimes happens that even dogs see fun as a reward.) For that reason, in my previous books, I used storytelling to convey certain messages and include what I wanted people to know and remember. This book will be different from the previous ones; however, I hope it will be interesting enough.

I

Why Are There So Many Therapies That Don't Work?

Have you ever been to therapy? Most of us have tried some form of therapy or perhaps self-help; if a person hasn't tried any of those, it doesn't mean they don't need them. As much as it seems that in the twenty-first century, we have seen an increase in mental health problems, it is also the time in which we don't have to be ashamed of those problems; in the civilized world, we are encouraged to seek help. That is a good thing. The bad thing is that many therapists see it as a great opportunity to simply make money, which is, of course, the wrong kind of motivation. Many psychology students just want the diploma so they can hang it in their office and start working and earning money – yet most of them are not willing to dive into real knowledge and keep learning as they go. You probably know what I am talking about; you must have seen it. Sticking to one type of therapy (usually the most popular at the moment) is a handicap; it limits the therapist and, as a result, the therapy itself. I have noticed that many therapists reject some pretty good ideas, claiming they are "old". Yes, some old ideas are bad, and it makes sense – when those hypotheses were formulated and tested, we knew so little, and psychology was just at its beginning. Some forms of therapy can be very bad and unethical. There are many bad ideas that professionals have accepted and followed in the past. However, there are many *new* ideas that are bad; they are not working, and the therapy turns out to be useless—even harmful (perhaps not harmful to one's mental health, but certainly harmful to their bank account). Another thing you must have noticed is the emergence of ridiculous therapies that are nothing but games for bored wealthy individuals who can afford to be fashionable even though nothing is really wrong in their lives. There are also people who are truly desperate and would try anything. But these therapies are just that – fashion. I have another word for them: nonsense. They are probably attractive not only because the other (bad) therapies didn't work but because they are "novel", and people in need don't lose hope easily. (Indeed, it is easier to lose money than hope.) Now, since those new therapies are marketed as something revolutionary, people have become curious. If they are pricey, that attracts people even more. In the era of consumerism, we are *manipulated* into thinking that more expensive *always* means better. As a result, the unfortunate and almost resigned client will do everything in their power to convince themselves that they, in fact, have not wasted their money (again!) and that therapy X, Y, or Z did, in fact, help. Consumerism culture, the silly need to keep up with "the trends," the lack of critical thinking, as well as the increase in mental health problems altogether created a special kind of absurdity; on several occasions, I had to explain to the people I was helping, that the fact that I am not charging them does not mean that my methods will not help them or that they are not worthy of our time and our joint efforts. I also remember something that happened many years ago, when I decided to make one of my books (as an e-book) free for a while. That took place in Serbia. Some people were happy about it and went on to download and read it. However, many people – way too many for my taste – started insulting both me and the book (even though they neither knew me nor have they read the book), saying that it "must be so bad, that no one wants to buy it, so I, the author, have to give the books away." Now if that is not poor thinking, I don't know what is. Still, that is the world we are living in. Things haven't changed that much since that moment (and that was in 2013).

I don't enjoy judging other therapists or people in general. However, when it comes to morality and ethics, it is hard for me to remain silent. I jokingly say that I lost a good friend to bad therapy. I haven't lost her; she is alive, and we are still friends, but she is not really getting better. She keeps suppressing her sadness, anger, and feelings of guilt. *She insists on a certain kind of (not very productive) therapy because that therapy allows her to avoid confronting "bad" emotions and painful memories.* The truth is, her problem could be resolved in less than a year if she only agreed to try a different method. However, in this case, as a loving friend, I will never criticize her choice of therapy; she is a lovely but somewhat stubborn person, so that would never work. All I can do in this case is be there whenever she needs a friend, not give my opinion unless asked, and not even try to influence her, since it would probably damage the friendship we have, and then I would not be able to help in any way whatsoever. Another reason why most therapies don't work is that some of them consist mostly of listening. The client speaks, and the therapist listens, nodding and taking notes. Now, let me say straight away that as a therapist, you must be a great listener. However, that should never be all that you do. You are there to listen when it is necessary, but only because it will provide you with the information you need to find the best type of therapy for that client. Have you noticed that people believe that "you will feel better after you have talked about it? I agree – but for that, you don't need to pay a therapist. You can talk to your friends, parents, and others who love and are close to you. Most of them will listen and even give you advice if you ask. You don't always go to a therapist in order to just "get it out of your system"; you go to a therapist for solutions. I repeat, listening is an important part of therapy, but it is not the only part. It works well when people really have no one else to talk to; it also helps the therapist gather more information – but all of that, ultimately, should help the therapist come up with real solutions and ensure the results are real and permanent. Furthermore, I noticed that many therapists rely too much on forms and questionnaires, trying to put a label on the client. I understand it is a tool that helps the professional gather as much information as possible about the client; however, this is not the type of work that can be done properly if one is overly dependent on classifications and categorizations. Lacking flexibility and relying more on the standardized questionnaires than on your own intuition, not having a quick and creative response, failing to perceive the client as a unique case (although there might be many similarities between clients and their problems, he/she is still a unique case!)—all that takes away a lot of your potential as a therapist. Go ahead and gather all the information you need; take notes—of course you will need them—but first and foremost: look at the person in front of you. There is one more thing I consider wrong and potentially dangerous: a professional who is too quick to prescribe medications. Just to be clear, I am not against medications; I simply think that they should be the last thing to try when everything else fails. There are certain conditions that simply cannot be managed without medications, and we should be grateful for having those medications; on the other hand, many mental health issues can and should be treated with psychotherapy and without medications. If all the different approaches prove to be fruitless, medication is the last resort. It can save lives, I agree. However, it can also destroy them. It is not only about the possible side effects; another problem lies in withdrawal. When treating depression and anxiety, for example (and in most cases, they come from some sort of trauma, whether the individual remembers it or not), it should be of the utmost importance that the therapist exhausts all the possible methods and approaches before a medication is prescribed. And if that happens, before the medication is prescribed, the professional must ensure it is safe for the client.

Sticking exclusively to one approach and one method is another reason why a therapist is likely to fail – unless, of course, you are the lucky client, and that specific approach happens to help you. However, it is unlikely to help *everyone*. (This is a good moment to point out that the method I will describe in this book is *not* for everyone, but it has proven effective many times in people with certain types of problems.)

If therapy hasn't helped a person within 2 years, it will most certainly not help at any time in the future. If a person has been in therapy for more than two years and that form of therapy hasn't helped, it means it simply doesn't work, and it is time for a different therapist. A while ago, one person told me, "Oh, I spent about two years in therapy with that therapist. She helped me a lot. Since then, I have tried different kinds of therapy, and soon I am going to try "that and that" therapy." "Really?" I thought to myself, "If your first therapy had worked, why are you looking for different therapies, still trying to resolve the same old problems?" In fact, I can tell you I am certain of one thing: If your therapy hasn't helped you in *less than one year*, you should look for a new therapist. **In fact, after the first six months of therapy, some results should already be evident, even if the client has only one session per week. That is twenty-four weeks, meaning twenty-four sessions. If there are no significant results after 24 sessions, it means the therapy and/or therapist are not successful.** Of course, the times will vary depending on what type of problem is being treated. I also do not believe that one session per week is sufficient, unless the client simply needs someone to talk to about casual things.

I couldn't help but notice that there are literally millions of people offering advice on YouTube. Many of them are professionals. I also noticed that the vast majority overcomplicate things when explaining something. They speak about "solutions", or they just put that word in the title of the video, but when you are done watching, you realize that the "solution" hasn't been offered at all. They usually offer vague advice that makes you either think, "Well, I know that already," or "What are they saying?". It almost seems as if they don't want to reveal the solution. Why would that be? Probably because they want you to contact them for sessions and give them your money. I promise things are much simpler than they seem when explained by those guys.

In this book, I will explain an eclectic method that I have never heard anyone else discuss. I have made use of many ideas I learned from the "old sources," adapting them to each case and combining them with the most recent discoveries, which seemed like the most logical approach in search of a method that could help a wide variety of cases.

II

Therapy – Guidance and Influence

What is psychotherapy?

We can agree that it is a process that uses various methods, usually based on personal interaction, aimed at helping a person overcome various kinds of problems and change their life for the better. How does a therapist do this? As you know, there are many kinds of therapies, but what do they all have in common? The objective is to influence the client so that they can improve their quality of life.

Yes – it is manipulation. As a therapist, you are going to influence (a nicer word for "manipulate") your client into thinking or feeling differently about him/herself, some event, or anything else that might be bothering them.

To be a good therapist means to successfully influence someone to help them (meaning being able to talk them into or out of thinking/feeling/doing something). How do you become one such therapist?

I believe it is, in a way, similar to becoming a good singer, athlete, or perhaps artist. You must have a certain kind of talent for it, and then you build on that talent as you grow, mature, and learn. In other words, there cannot be great success without talent, nor can there be success without learning, practice, and a commitment to improvement.

What tools do you need to be a good therapist?

As you can imagine, you have to be a **good listener**. Unfortunately, many therapists give too much space to passive listening; they believe that the client will feel better if he/she speaks about the problem. This is correct, especially in cases where a person has absolutely no one to talk to. However, listening alone is far from sufficient, and the therapy should include many other elements. It is necessary (and useful) to listen—this is how you gather information. Asking a question here and there is another useful tool; still, focusing too much on completing questionnaires and taking notes will not be too helpful in the long run. Those tools are only there to help you offer a solution as soon as possible.

You have to be able to **ask the right questions at the right moment**, using the right intonation and the right words. Your question must be perfectly formulated if you want to understand the person in front of you and gain their trust. Which brings me to the next thing:

Knowing how to use **facial expressions** and **intonation in your voice,** and knowing what kind of person you have in front of you, will be of great help. You will know how to position yourself and how to approach the client. It is safe to say that a single session will be sufficient for a skilled therapist to understand the client's personality and the problems they are facing. In less than one hour, you will know what is expected from you and what your client needs, whether they tell you that or not. Now, how can you know these things? Remember what I said before: talent + knowledge + experience.

Your **client must feel safe** when talking to you. You have to radiate confidence and competence. You have to be certain that you can help your client. How, you will ask, can I be certain? Well, that depends on your talent, knowledge, and experience. The more of those three you have, the more confident you will be, and your client will sense it. It is contagious in a way. As I mentioned, your client must feel safe not only while talking to you; your job is to influence them so they feel safe *after* they leave your office. **Never underestimate** the magnitude that the client's problem has (for them) or the power it has over them. Of course, many therapists fall into that trap, out of the very best intentions – to yank the client out of his misery, they start telling him/her that there are many "worse" problems out there and if they look around, they will see it is true and start feeling better. Even though this might be the truth in many cases, saying that to your client is a very bad idea. It will not help at all; instead, it will create distance between you. Speaking of distance, you don't need to act as your client's close **friend**; however, your client needs to *feel* as if you are. Talking about your private life is not something you should be doing, but if your client asks you something and you feel that answering that question cannot do harm to either of you, go ahead and answer. You will look like a human being rather than something impersonal and faceless – and that is a good thing. If you want to avoid answering a question, saying, "We are not here to talk about me; we are here for you", or "I can't answer that question," is *not* the way to go. Formulate your answer in a different, friendly way, and move away from the question. Making a joke at your expense without giving out details is a very good way to handle this type of situation.

Your intuition (or call it talent) will always be on, like a background process. It must be there at all times, not just during the initial sessions. Thanks to this, you will know when to change the strategy, what to do, and how to do it. Combine this with knowledge and experience, and you will have great chances of succeeding, no matter how complicated the task may be.

Empathy is one of the most important tools you will ever have. You will say, "But empathy is a gift; it is not a tool". Of course it is a gift, and of course it is a tool. I dare go so far as to say that *if not used as a tool, then is not a gift at all*. If you can use it to put yourself in another person's shoes, do it – even though you might suffer a bit during the process, feeling what the other person is feeling. "But I don't want to suffer", you will say. Of course not. Nobody wants to suffer. However, you are a human being, and if you have empathy, it is normal to be touched by another person's situation. Don't fear it; once you help that person, you will see it was worth it. I am not saying you should become depressed if your client suffers from depression – let us not take it to extremes. I believe you understand what I am trying to say. If you know yourself and your job, you will be able to regulate your own feelings quite well, and your empathy will not turn on you. It will become your ally.

Forget vanity. As soon as we accept that we don't know everything, we will start improving. There is always a new challenge, a new opportunity to learn and grow, and new ways of doing things.

III

Trauma

The word *trauma* literally means "wound". It can also mean "defeat". In psychology, trauma is defined as a response to a bad event. Trauma is not measured by an objective scale of the gravity of bad events; it is measured by the consequences those events have had on an individual (or sometimes a large group; in that case, it is called "collective trauma"). You will see that different people are affected differently by the same event; the way they respond does not depend on the event itself as much as on their personalities, shaped by genetics and their personal histories. Psychological trauma can manifest not only as a mental and emotional problem; it often manifests in the form of physical illness or pain, as well as various problems in different organs of the body. The job of the therapist is not to treat symptoms but to treat the cause. This is one of the reasons medications should not be prescribed as quickly as they are today. I agree that in some cases, when there is no other way, medications can save lives. However, these drugs carry their own risks, and not taking those risks into consideration is a dangerous and irresponsible thing to do. I have met many people who take medications to treat depression and/or anxiety without having had any kind of serious psychotherapy; this is an example of trying to camouflage the problem by addressing the symptoms instead of focusing on the cause. Sometimes, the consequences of trauma can be so horrible that the person can't function at all, and it is tempting to start taking medications. I repeat, I am not arguing that medications should never be prescribed; I am arguing that they are not sufficient – not in the long run. Until the cause is dealt with in another way, there will be no real improvement. Remember, the client will have to stop taking the medication *eventually*.

As we know, trauma does not only affect the person in question; it affects everyone else in that person's life, and that is how it makes things even worse for the unfortunate individual. It takes a toll on their relationships and, as a result, makes them feel even worse due to the feeling of guilt, inadequacy, low self-worth, and many other "demons".

Trauma, as we know, is a complex problem. This is why I cannot stress the importance of being open to different kinds of therapies and approaches. Remember: in this field, one size *never* fits all.

We could imagine unresolved trauma as a wound that never heals; it keeps opening, and every time it opens, someone puts some salt on it. Not only can the wound not heal, but it sometimes gets worse. Treating it can be a lengthy, painful, and turbulent process; an important part of the therapist's job is to make that process less painful. When speaking about trauma, I said many times that we can't change the past; what we can change, however, is the way we feel about it. Memories, including traumatic ones, are nothing but mental photographs; they have no power outside of the self. Their power lies in the way we feel about them. The answer is not to "forget" or suppress; in many cases, it is, in fact, impossible to forget a traumatic event. Training your mind and body to respond *differently* is the only solution. Refusing to think about something, trying to escape, or desperately trying to distract yourself – those are nothing but small, superficial "fixes", with short-lasting effects.

Confronting the problem, accepting it, and then working towards taking control of your emotions and your way of responding to a traumatic event from the past – that, in my opinion, is the only way.

IV

What Is the Separation Method?

I would like to start off by explaining what the "separation method" is *not*.

The method I will describe in this book can be used on people over twenty-five and "fully" adult individuals. Children and toddlers will not respond to it, and it is highly unlikely to have any effect on an adolescent. There are several reasons why the therapist's approach will depend on the client's age. For example, adolescents process information primarily with the amygdala; they feel things much more than they think about them or think them through. They are not very good at observing things objectively, and they often cannot properly understand or define their own emotions (or thoughts). Adults use the prefrontal cortex, the part of the brain in charge of "rational thinking," impulse control, consequence assessment, and judgment, which is a huge difference compared to an adolescent brain. Therefore, adolescents are, in a way, "hard work" – for the parents as well as for the therapists, counselors, psychologists, and life coaches. It is extremely important to understand what is happening in the adolescent's life; failing to do so can have serious, sometimes tragic consequences. It is not very hard to reach an adolescent for a short period of time, to "click" with them and get them to open up, but that doesn't mean much. Working with teenagers is almost like a full-time job. You, as someone who is trying to help, will have to be available whenever you are needed – even when the teenager thinks that he/she doesn't need you.

When it comes to the time of the client's life when a traumatic event occurred, we will agree that it is a *very* important factor. Babies, toddlers, children, adolescents, and adults will all respond differently simply because their brains differ. A good professional will, of course, know how to approach a client no matter when his trauma has occurred. Some clients will not remember the traumatic experience itself, but they will still be suffering from trauma. This makes a therapist's work a bit more complex. A baby can't form memories simply because the part of the brain in charge of the formation of memories is not yet developed. If the trauma occurred when your client was a baby or toddler, it means that you will have to use different techniques to get to the bottom of it; your client may not remember something, but there are other things about him/her that will be quite indicative.

Let us now go back to what the "separation method" is not.

It is not a miracle. Just like other methods in any kind of therapy, it will not work for everyone. There are problems that simply cannot be resolved using this method alone. Nevertheless, it will be helpful as a part of the therapy; it certainly cannot do harm. However, it will not always be sufficient. Mental illnesses such as schizophrenia, for example, cannot be successfully treated using this method. It can only be used as a small part of the therapy, but most likely, it will not resolve the issue.

It cannot treat "heavy" addictions (still, it will be a useful tool during therapy).

It might not *completely* resolve problems such as post-traumatic stress disorder, although it can help immensely.

It cannot resolve problems such as borderline personality disorder, for example. It can, however, be a useful tool during the initial phases of therapy.

Finally, the "separation method" is not in any way threatening to lead to another disorder in a client. You will guess, the disorder I am talking about is depersonalization-derealization disorder. The "separation method" is a mental exercise that lasts only minutes or even seconds, and it is meant to help the client resolve past issues so they can return to themselves and live a better life. By no means should the client be encouraged or taught to exist as a separate personality. The "separation" is used **ONLY** as an exercise to help the person see their situation objectively and help themselves, not as a means of separating from themselves too frequently or permanently. To be more specific, in the "separation method", the person is not "divorced" from themselves or their feelings, and they are not trying to *feel their problems* as if they were happening to another human being. Quite the contrary.

Furthermore, what used to seem "hazy" becomes very clear, allowing the client to understand, accept, and change it. Dissociation and depersonalization are usually a response to a severely traumatic experience, and they serve as a way of escape. In the "separation", the goal is quite the opposite – to confront things that caused the trauma and *start feeling differently about them.* As we know, dissociation and depersonalization diminish pretty much all the experience, not only the traumatic one; it is a *disorder* that has nothing to do with the "separation method." The "separation method" is a short mental exercise. It is a means to quickly regulate one's own feelings and take control, preventing harmful sentiments from taking over. This is done by viewing the situation as an observer, allowing the person to see it objectively and often realizing that it *doesn't feel as bad as it seems.* When you finish reading this book, all of this will be clear to you. In fact, as strange as it may sound to you now, the separation method can be used to help clients with depersonalization-derealization disorder. When you finish reading this book, you will understand why and how.

The separation method is carefully composed of a series of exercises, and the therapist guides the client through each of those. It looks like hypnosis or can even resemble a type of meditation; however, it is neither of those things.

Why do I call it the "separation method"?

The very essence of this method is a mental exercise in which one "separates from him/herself" (only during the mental exercise, of course). What do I mean by that?
The session consists of a relatively short conversation between you and the client to gather information about their problem and history; this will become clear once I give a few examples later in the book. At this point, let's say that you, the therapist, know that your client suffers from childhood trauma.

You will ask about the event or the events that caused the trauma (if the client remembers them). If the client does not remember the events that caused the trauma, you can dive into his/her past and ask about the client's worst memories.

An experienced therapist will easily determine which of the client's memories to use in the session and for future mental exercises. This will become clearer further in the book when I describe a few examples. The most important thing is to get to know your client well and be proactive rather than just a passive listener. When I say, "the client will separate from him/herself," what does that really mean for them? It means that you will bring your client back to the moment the traumatic event occurred, and he/she will observe the situation from the outside, as a bystander, *not* as a participant. They will be able to see the person who, at that moment, was, in fact, themselves, but from the outside, *not as themselves*.

There are also a number of mental exercises that you will teach your client, and you will explain to him/her when and how to do them. We will get to those further in the book.

How do you bring the client into this state of relaxation and focus? You can guess – you will use one of the several techniques of relaxation. You will lead your client to physically relax to the point where he/she can focus only on the situation (from the past, when the bad event occurred) into which you are sending her/him. You will guide the client and maintain their focus on the situation. Your client cannot do this on their own; you have to guide them every step of the way. While your client is "back in the past" as an observer, what you say to them and *how* you say it is extremely important. As I said, when the client is "back in the past", they will be watching the event from the outside, as a spectator, and they will see their "old" self, who was somehow involved in the event. What makes this method nonsense-free is the simple fact that your client *now*, indeed, *is* a different person than they were in the past. When you teach your client to "separate from himself," you are not lying or telling your client fairy tales; in fact, the truth is that your client truly is a different person than he/she was before. And this "new" person has to go back in time and change something for the "old" person. No one else can do it, and no one else *should*.

There are likely to be tears at first, of course. However, your job is to train your client to gradually start feeling differently, and that is achieved through practice. Repeating one or more mental exercises at the right moments will lead to this: your client will start feeling differently about their "old" self and, eventually, about the others involved in the event and the event itself.

Your client needs to learn the exercise and repeat it whenever he/she encounters the feelings that are tormenting them. With time, as he/she learns the exercise well, your client will reach the point where it will only take a few seconds for their feelings to change – it will become almost instant; they will train their mind and body to feel differently about an event or a person, and after a while, before too long, the client will become free of pain. The pain or other problematic feelings will be entirely replaced by a sense of accomplishment, strength, and, ultimately, peace. A traumatic event cannot be erased from the past, but the trauma caused by it can and must be resolved. The key is changing the way your client feels about the event. That will heal the wound. That will also liberate them in many other ways, and all the behaviors and problems that stem from that trauma will be resolved with your help. Why is it crucial that the client "gets out of himself" for a few minutes or seconds? The explanation is very logical. We are great at helping others; we can see very clearly what is wrong in their lives or in specific situations because we are observing them from the outside. It helps us be objective; we see things clearly. When we are looking at our own problems, they usually seem more complicated or worse than they are because we are subjective and caught up in our feelings. Has it ever happened to you that you could give perfect advice to someone, you knew exactly what that person should do, and you even managed to help them – but when it came to you and your own problems, you were stuck? We are often better at helping others than helping ourselves. That is why one needs to "get out of oneself" – to be able to observe oneself as if it were someone else – someone who needs *their* help.

I remember helping people even when I was not doing great. My capacity to help them had nothing to do with how I felt about my problems or their gravity. Why was that so? Because I was helping someone else. How many times have you been told that you take care of others much more easily and better than you take care of yourself? Be honest, how many times – can you even count? Your job is to lead your client to truly feel, for a moment, that there is *that other person* who lives in the past and is suffering and needs help. It is very important for the client to be the one who will help "that other person" because that is what your client needs. You want him/her to be responsible, and you want to empower them. It is not you who will help "the other person from the past"; it is your client who will do it himself/herself. This will make them feel responsible, strong, and empowered, and those sentiments are necessary for the future progress your client will make in many other areas. It will also help them stop seeing themselves as the victim and instead see themselves as their own savior – because that is literally what they will be doing –

saving "the other person from the past" – their past self.

What I do, and I haven't seen many coaches and therapists do, is try to be available to the client even if they don't have an appointment. I am not saying you should cancel other appointments, but you can tell your client that they can send you a message, and you will read it or listen to it and respond when you can. Your client cannot predict when they will feel bad and when they will need help. At the beginning of the therapy, your client does not know how to do the "separation" exercises. They are just beginners, and they still depend on you since you clearly have more knowledge of the subject. In the early stages of the therapy, they are your responsibility. Yes, you have the right to rest and relax; however, you are the one who is (more or less) fine, and they are not. When your client learns how to use this tool, they will need you less and less. However, in the early stages of the therapy, they might need you when they feel bad or lost. The way I see it, your job is to be there, even if it interrupts your dinner. Your dinner is there, waiting for you. Things will change, and you will not always have to be there; however, during the first month (or two, depending on the case), you might need to be there when your client needs you. This usually doesn't take longer than ten minutes. It doesn't mean that the client will become too dependent on you. In fact, you will be there when your client needs you to guide them and help them learn the exercise properly, so they can become less and less dependent on you.

To resume, with proper work, your client will begin to:

• see himself/herself as *another person* who needs *their* help
• see things in an objective way

- feel empowered to step in and help because that is what he/she would do for another person in need
- feel responsibility for the past self instead of blaming other people (even though they (other people) might be the ones to blame for the traumatic event). It is important to distinguish between those – yes, someone else was responsible and guilty, but now the client is responsible for resolving it because now he/she has the power to fight back and take their life back into their own hands. Blaming others, even though they are as guilty as can be, will never resolve anything. On the contrary, it will only enable the client to keep living as a victim forever.
- feel satisfaction after a few sessions when they master the mental exercise that you will teach them

• learn how to train not just their mind but also their body to feel differently about certain events or persons from the past. Their mind *and* body will start to feel different, thanks to practice. It is a matter of habit; for many years, the client has been accustomed to responding to a bad event (and the people involved) in a certain way. Your job is to change those ways. It takes some time, but not too long. In addition, your client will learn the exercise (s) and will be able to do them independently when necessary, becoming less dependent on you.

I have seen many therapists try to convince their clients that they must not live in the past and must look to the future. That is one of the most unprofessional and inhumane things a professional can do. It is not only insensitive but also ignorant. How can anyone focus on the future if they are carrying the heavy, painful weight of their past every moment of their lives, and it keeps affecting everything they do, including the future they are trying to create for themselves and their families?

What information do you need the most from your client? Start at the very beginning – their parents, even their grandparents, and then their early years. Childhood holds explanations for pretty much everything. Even if a person experienced some sort of trauma when they were an adult, the way they lived as a child will determine how the traumatic event affected them and how they responded to it as adults. This information will help you see better how this person processed the trauma. Healthy kids grow up to be healthy adults, or at least adults well equipped to deal with life's traumas and difficulties. Furthermore, you need to know *what* happened – sometimes, it is impossible to know this because the client himself is not aware of it or doesn't remember it. If that is the case, you will need to consider the symptoms and difficulties your client is currently experiencing.

Help the client identify the issues. You are only there to guide them, not to tell them what to think about themselves or about an event. You are there to help them understand themselves and their problems, not to sit them down and explain things to them as if they were in primary school.

During the "separation" exercise, encourage the person to speak out loud. Hearing their own voice will be of great help in the process of training and "reprogramming" the mind and the body.

Encourage your client to take notes about how they feel and the circumstances in which certain feelings occur. They should try to identify what they are feeling. These notes will be helpful to you and your client.

Thanks to the "separation method," I have seen great results in people who suffered from depression and anxiety (those usually come from trauma); however, it can be used in individuals who are struggling with addictions or other problems – not as the only approach, but as a useful tool. If you, for some reason, are not getting good results, it means you have to study harder. By "study," I don't mean only study this method; I also mean *study your client*. Another thing you should always be doing is improving your skills as a therapist or life coach, but you already know that.

I believe I have left some things unfinished in this chapter. You are probably wondering why I didn't explain how to bring the client into the right state in which he/she can focus on the traumatic event and "separate from themselves for a few minutes".

Also, some of you, while reading this book, might have been wondering, "Where is the catch? Why is she revealing all of this for all of us to use, just like that?" Well, here comes the catch. I will not tell you how to bring the person into the proper state in which the separation method will work (I am referring to both physical relaxation and mental focus).

Here is why:
1. If you are a good and knowledgeable therapist or life coach, you will know how to do this—I don't even have to tell you.
2. If you don't know how to do it, then you probably should not be using this method in the first place.

3. If you don't know how to do it, it will be a great learning opportunity for you. You will have to read all that you can find – including the books that date back to the early beginnings – and then, you will practice until you know enough to bring a person into a state of real physical relaxation as well as mental focus, in order to use this method.

Please don't be offended by what I just said. I am simply trying to share something with you, not forgetting – not even for a moment – the responsibility I have for *your* clients.

V

A Few Stories

I would like to start off with a story that confirms several things: 1. The only person who cannot be helped is the person who doesn't want to be helped. 2. Without sufficient knowledge and experience, even if your intentions are nothing but good, you can help only to a certain extent, and it will likely be insufficient.…3. The therapies that are used for drug addictions in some parts of the world are very limited, one-sided, and rigid, even cruel. That is why they don't work in the long run. They are all about isolating the client, separating the client from his drug of choice, and replacing it with another (legal) drug. The element that is missing here is the client him/herself. Getting to *truly* know the client through psychotherapy is usually missing. The "separation method" can be very helpful during psychotherapy, although I am not arguing that it will be sufficient. In addition, there is a risk that the client will become too dependent on you, the therapist. Addicts usually seek to replace one addiction with another. Your job is to enable the client to try to help himself, which is extremely hard in cases of addiction, where people seek "help" and a quick "solution" in something that is not inside them, but somewhere else (in this case, it is drugs).

I have a story about this.

When I was around twenty-one (still a university student), something tragic happened to my distant cousins. Our families used to be close when we were small, but over time, they grew apart. That family had two sons. The older one became an IV drug user, and soon enough, he managed to lure his younger brother into using and dealing drugs as well. The younger one was my age. I will call him "the cousin."

We had lost touch, and as I knew what they were doing (I mean, drugs), I preferred not to be in contact with them. One day, the older brother overdosed and died. The younger one was still young, and even though his problem was severe, there was, in theory, still some hope for him, especially after the death of his brother - one would think that would be a wake-up call. Well, not really, as you will see later in the story.

I heard the sad news, and I remembered how we used to play when we were children. My cousin used to be a gymnast, a very good boy, in fact. He was very different from his older brother. I felt sorry for him, and I wanted to help. I showed up out of nowhere, trying to offer support and help. At the time, I was studying in another city.

Before that, I had never had contact with drug addicts. I did not know enough about it; all I wanted was to help this person. I invited him to Belgrade to study and resume sports; I thought it would be good to separate him from the harmful people he was hanging out with. I thought, "If this person is in a different environment, with new, constructive tasks, and if he puts some effort into that, he will slowly get used to normal life. Also, it is not so easy to get drugs in a place where you don't know absolutely anyone and anything." Or at least, that was what I thought.

Before starting college, which I had talked him into doing, he went to a ten-day rehab. Of course, it wasn't sufficient. When he completed it, I offered him a place to stay at my rental, thinking he could use the company and that I would also be able to keep an eye on him and help in difficult moments.

During that year, he improved. He stopped taking drugs—or at least, he stopped taking heavy drugs. However, he became very dependent on me; he almost seemed jealous whenever I had to go out of town, such as for university seminars. I was very busy, and I was not prepared to care for him twenty-four-seven. It became extremely difficult to live like that for both of us. We agreed that he should find a place of his own, and it was for the best. He chose to go back to where his parents lived, and you can guess – he went back to drugs. After that, I heard that he went to another kind of rehab – offered by the church, and based on religious brainwashing, without professional help or anyone to guide him through the process. In that way, he unfortunately ended up placing the responsibility in God's hands rather than his own.

I realized that he only wanted help when I was there, pushing help and being occupied with him at all times. I should have paid attention to that. However, that was my first experience with a heavy drug user; although I knew some things, I was still young and inexperienced. I did my best because I did it from the heart, but I learned the hard way that "the heart" was not enough. The relationship with my cousin had become very unhealthy, and that was something to be expected. I am glad I managed to resolve those problems in a peaceful and relatively painless way; still, none of it had to happen. It only happened because I was kind-hearted, unwilling to give up, hopeful, and poorly informed – therefore unprepared. In his case, the "separation method" would not have worked. When I started helping him, he was too self-destructive, too broken, and completely lost.

The "separation method", however, would have worked after the year we spent together as a part of the therapy; by that time, he had restored some of his self-love and the will to live a normal life. Had he avoided the "church rehab" and sought real, serious professional help, his chances would have been better.

Here is a success story. It is about a troubled mother and her daughter. The mother had a very unhealthy upbringing; her own mom was an abusive, rather primitive woman who always loved her son better than her daughter. She was unpleasant, offensive, and sometimes extremely physically aggressive towards the little girl. You can guess what happened to that little girl. She grew up to be an insecure individual, seeking to be saved, looking for someone who would spoil her (her need to be loved was unfulfilled to the extent that she needed extreme expressions of love; that is why she wanted to be spoiled by someone – anyone). She grew to think that it was other people's responsibility to always take care of her and that she was entitled to it, which persisted into her later life and never changed. Throughout her life, she felt that no one loved, understood, supported, or appreciated her, and she was angry with the whole world, always disappointed. She had the constant need to somehow place herself above others. Her friendships were shallow and short-lasting, and she would always end up feeling hurt and abandoned. She never thought she needed any kind of professional help; in her mind, she was perfect, and everyone else was flawed and wrong. She never developed the healthy ability to acknowledge her flaws, mistakes, or problems. Instead, her choice was to deny everything she didn't like about herself; her ability to face reality was nonexistent. You will guess she became emotionally abusive towards her own family – her husband and her own small daughter. That little girl lived in a very unhappy home; she did, however, spend time with her paternal grandparents, who were by no means a perfect example of a happy couple; however, she never *saw* crying or abuse in the grandparents' home. That was a better alternative to her own home, where the mother was crying and insulting everyone every day, including her small daughter. It is very upsetting for a young child to see her primary caregiver distressed, in constant pain, and tears. The mother's job is to provide safety, love, protection, and nourishment. Simply put, her mom failed at those things. There was, however, her father, who spent time with her, doing fun things together; there was her grandfather too. When she was still a young girl, her mother gave birth to a boy. You will guess what happened. The mother started to behave exactly like her own mother did when *she* was small. The boy was treated like a deity, and the girl was pushed aside, always blamed for things that had nothing to do with her whatsoever. The mother created a "clan" within the family; the only members were her new baby boy and herself. I believe this continues to this very day, even though everyone is a grown-up. Ironically, she is aware of her own mother's behavior and its catastrophic consequences, yet she has done the exact same thing. Only this time, things went in a different direction for her daughter; she realized that was not a way to live or feel, and she worked hard to heal and not follow the patterns that ran in her family. She had a choice: she could either leave things as they were, her old wounds unhealed, and suffer – or she could address her own pain from the past and learn how to feel differently about her mother and the things her mother had done or was still doing.

The "separation method" worked perfectly for that young woman. Once she learned how to look at things as a spectator, she realized that it wasn't her fault that she could not stop her mother from crying; it wasn't her fault that the mother was unhappy; it was not her job to take care of her mother – it was the other way around. Using the "separation method" exercises, she would successfully "go back in time" and take that little girl out of the stressful situations, one by one. **This is just one example of the exercises that this method uses. There are more of these exercises, and they differ depending on each case.** Now, you will ask me: "How did she take the little girl out?" When she went back (in her mind) to a traumatic situation, she took the girl by her hand, felt the little girl's hand in hers, and took her out. She told her something to make her feel better. She truly convinced the little girl that everything was going to get better. She would say it out loud: "You are safe. Life will not be like this". She would then repeat this exercise every time she felt sad about the past; she would relax, close her eyes, and feel the girl's hand in her hand. She would then smile, each time reminded that she had saved that little girl, and she was now safe. Is this a lie? No. The woman really is not that girl anymore; she is now safe and strong. When she said to that little girl (in her thoughts) that things would change, she didn't lie. Things *did* change; the woman even managed to "go back" and "save" the girl. Now, let's explain this a bit better. Why is it important to "travel back in time" and resolve the problem that occurred in the past? And why was this exercise so important? The goal is not to erase a bad memory - that little girl did exist. However, the goal is to train the mind and body to feel differently about it. We are creating a new image and a new sentiment (for example, an image of a little girl being "saved"). With time, that sentiment will overpower the old feelings of pain, sadness, hopelessness, and guilt. In the beginning, your client will probably cry a lot, but with a bit of time and practice, the client will not cry during the exercise anymore. He/she will start to feel calm and empowered. In this case, the image of the little girl being safe has taken hold in the woman's mind, and she no longer associates the little girl (and childhood memories) with pain but with a different sentiment – the one we created together.

She was successfully trained to feel differently not only about the past but also about the present. Her mother never changed, but the woman changed the way she felt about her mother, her words, and her actions. And what followed was perfectly logical: she broke the pattern! Today, she is a great mother to her child, living in a peaceful home with no shouting, tears, drama, insults, or any form of emotional abuse. Her relationship with her younger brother is loving; they are close and always support each other. All the other things she could see in her mother's behavior when she (the subject) was a child, that she was worried she would perhaps repeat in her adult life, are simply not there.

The process was not easy, but it worked, and the results were permanent. She changed her *habit* of feeling/acting one way (reacting with pain, sadness, and guilt) and replaced it with new sentiments and a new way of *feeling things* and looking at herself, her mother, her past, the present, and the future.

The next story is about a boy from a poor family. His father was a construction worker, and his mother was a stay-at-home mom. They lived in a poor country devastated by civil war. Clearly, this family of five was accustomed to living in a stressful environment, struggling to survive. The father was drinking too much; I suspect he was trying to fill a void; he also craved the company of others – the house was always full, chaotic, and noisy. His parenting style included beating his three small children, and occasionally, he would beat his wife as well. When this little boy grew up, surprisingly enough, his mental health was not *too* bad. He grew up to be a good person, sensitive to others' needs. As a young adult, he seems to have a fine relationship with both his parents. The circumstances had changed; the family had relocated to another country, and the father seemed to have abandoned some of his old ways. However, in his close relationships, the young man displayed insecurities: he had trouble trusting others, was always doubting everyone, and often felt guilt and shame. It was just at the time when the "intervention" started that he was beginning to display his insecurities in a rather toxic manner, trying to control his partner, what she would wear, where she would go; he would become jealous not only of other men as competition but also of her female friends. This person apparently needed to get the right kind of attention; he also needed to learn what a healthy relationship was. In addition, he had to learn that it was not his fault that his family was dysfunctional and to accept that he, as a small child, could not have changed anything during those stressful moments he had witnessed. As a child, he had a lucky circumstance: he spent a lot of time with his neighbors – a young, childless couple. Watching a woman very different from his own mother go about her life in a way very different from his mom's was a good thing. When I met him, it was just the right time to start working on the issues and help him learn critical thinking, as well as to become more objective and introspective. He also had to learn how to regulate the destructive feelings of insecurity and/or guilt. In other words, he would have to learn what true freedom was.

In cases like this, the "separation method" is helpful since the person is not too young. However, young age, in general, often means a lack of introspection; it involves different hormonal activity and a reduced capacity to regulate emotions; in addition, the brain is not yet fully developed, and you, as a life coach or therapist, will be limited by all these factors. The closer the person is to the age of twenty-five, the more chances of succeeding you have as a life coach/therapist/counselor.

Now, here is a different kind of story. I believe this will be useful to all the parents out there. It is not about any kind of traumatic experience; it is about how I decided to adapt and use the "separation" technique in order to be a better mother to my son with autism. Let me first make a very short intro. My son was a healthy, "normal" baby; he would interact in a rather normal "baby way" and never displayed any difficulties, not even with sleep. Then, when he was around a year and a half, I noticed a change. He wouldn't interact as before; he didn't point, and he didn't say any words anymore. By the time he turned two, I was positive that something was simply different and not in a good way. We began our long, stressful journey from one professional to another. It was truly devastating, especially because no one was certain of anything they said; they all agreed that he "might have autism", but no one was offering any solutions. We tried all sorts of therapies, and nothing seemed to have changed his mind regarding communication. He *could* speak; he simply *didn't care* to. Seven years later, he still doesn't talk much, but he can speak three languages (when he really wants to). He understands pretty much everything, although he is still struggling to understand why social interactions are important. He is becoming more aware of his environment and the outside world in general, but those are still baby steps. The only thing I can say with certainty is that there is no way of predicting what the next phase in his development will bring. He went through phases of liking something, then not being able to stand something (sometimes it was the very same thing!); he went through phases of seeking attention in a rather strange way, one could even say "annoying way" – such as throwing objects, breaking them, even taking his pants off and peeing on the floor – all along laughing like crazy. He thought it was fun; he thought that would create a reaction and get him the kind of attention he needed at that moment. And it did prompt a reaction at school—his assistant and his educator were not thrilled by his mischievous behavior. When this first started, I thought it was just a one-time thing; "it will not happen again", I naively thought. As my son was proving me wrong almost every day, I realized I had to make a strategy. How could I fix this? It was not about the broken things (his favorite thing to break was glass); what bothered me was that no one had a solution. Needless to say, I was quite annoyed that this was happening to us. Imagine your child peeing on the floor a few times a day, every day, and then going on to throw and break whatever he could find – for fun! I am sure you wouldn't be enjoying it. Neither was I.

During that year, I spent several months trying everything I could think of as long as it wasn't harmful to my child. Nothing worked. I felt I had exhausted all the ideas on my list. Naturally, I became exhausted, too. After those few months of trying different things and failing, I realized that this phase might last longer than I thought. It was time to find a strategy to "fix" how I felt about it rather than to keep trying to "fix" my son's naughty behavior. And his behavior at that point was just one of the many things that were preventing me from doing activities such as sleeping, writing, going outside, and talking to other people (yes, he had a phase where he didn't want people around him to speak to each other!); I could not even see a movie, for example – he wouldn't let me watch anything on my laptop. I was literally spending all my time watching him so he wouldn't hurt himself and cleaning up the mess he made. If you imagine it as a movie, the background music would be the loud noises of a screaming child mixed with extremely loud, distorted noises he was playing on YouTube. It is safe to say that I, at the very least, was not feeling OK. I had to find a way to be happy – genuinely happy – and calm. I don't believe in corporal punishment; in fact, I don't believe that any kind of punishment is a good way of raising children. I had to find a way not to become angry at my child, the universe, or anyone else during those difficult moments. I tried my best (and succeeded) to be calm on the outside, not to shout or even speak – but that was only on the outside. Inside of me, there was an active volcano. I didn't want that volcano. I knew it would destroy me, and I could not afford that; my son needed me to be healthy and happy.

One day, I thought to myself: "Why not use the "separation technique"? Adapt it to your case, create the right exercise, and just do it". And so, I did. It worked perfectly; it never failed, not even once. People who visited us at home would often be shocked not only by my son's "crazy" behavior but also by the fact that I never got angry or annoyed. I would hug my kid, give him a kiss, wait till he calmed down, and peacefully go on to clean up the mess (I really don't like a mess or any kind of chaos; the house must always be clean and chaos-free. Imagine, then, the frustration I was going through every time he would make a total mess, and that was – every day).

I wish to share this with all the parents out there. What I did was the following:

• when my son starts with problematic behavior (that I can't prevent or stop), I stop whatever I am doing.

• I don't say a word, I don't make a move – this is extremely important.

• I look at the wall, focusing on one spot. I use one of my techniques to relax my body.

• Next, I look at the situation from the outside, and I see a kid who is happy even though he is doing "crazy stuff". I see a mother who loves her kid more than she is annoyed by his behavior. And, looking at the crazy stuff he does as a mere observer, I realize it is actually funny. If it were a movie, I would probably laugh a bit.

• I smile. Putting a smile on your face will send a message from your body to your mind: "I (the body) am smiling; therefore, everything must be well. If it weren't good, I wouldn't be smiling." This is just one of the ways you can train yourself to feel differently than you did before, when your "reflex" was to get angry and go "crazy" yourself.

• I hold my child, kiss him, and tell him I love him.

• Then, when I see it is "safe", I clean up.
The whole thing used to last a few minutes at first. Then, as my self-training went on, the time was reduced to a few seconds. Now I don't have to do these exercises at all. I have successfully trained my body and my mind to feel differently, and it is automatic. If I hadn't, my apparent calmness would have been nothing but an attempt to suppress my anger and frustration, and we know why suppressed feelings are bad and what *inevitably* happens in one's life (and the lives of one's family members) as a consequence of such feelings.

Eventually, this phase in my son's behavior finished. I always knew it would pass; however, I had to stay sane while it was happening!

Once I saw and felt the amazing change this method had made, I started applying it to everything else: dog training (as you know, it is all about being truly calm and patient. You can't lie to dogs; they just know when you're losing it), communication with other people whenever there is a problem and communication with myself, whenever I saw that I was about to start feeling something that was harmful to me or my family.

My life hasn't been easy since I turned ten, I think. That is a story for another book, though. Even though I managed to improve my life greatly, it certainly became hard when my son's symptoms started to occur; in addition, there were other things that were killing me day by day, but that would be a story too long to tell now. Either way, you get the picture.

Thanks to the "separation technique", I have literally saved myself from years-long misery (and by that, I mean misery), which was eating me alive and taking a huge toll on everything I was doing or trying to do. I recovered from a serious depression (without having taken a single medication), left toxic relationships, removed toxic people from my life, and went back to doing what I always enjoyed doing; I improved as a mother, as a person, and as my own friend.

VI

Why The Separation Method Works

Here are a few reasons why this method works.

• It is based on several theories, all of which have been proven correct. You cannot use an assumption if it hasn't been proven correct. If you do that, by adding a flawed element into a system, you might make the entire system flawed.
• It works because it is flexible and adaptable to different cases. That is precisely why not everyone can learn how to apply it. As I said before, almost like singing, you don't **only** need enough information, formal education, and book knowledge – you also need talent and intuition.
• It works because a person (or at least most people) knows exactly what to do when they see someone else in trouble. It also helps a person be more objective.

• It works because it helps a person feel responsible for someone or something and gives them a feeling of power and accomplishment.

• How many times have you said, after viewing a video of yourself: "Oh, I really look ridiculous. If I had known that I looked so ridiculous, I wouldn't have done that"? Or let's say you said something that hurt another person's feelings – perhaps you couldn't see it then because you were not that other person. However, when you step back and take a look at the situation objectively, you can see the things you had done wrong, and then, of course, you wish you hadn't. The "separation method" is a useful exercise for all of us. It is designed to help us in different situations. The goal is not only to resolve problems caused by trauma; for those who are trauma-free (if such people exist!), the goal is to avoid making mistakes you will later regret.

• It works because we are all creatures of habit. Change the habit of feeling a certain way about something, and you will have changed everything else connected to it. Training your mind and body to start feeling differently about something or someone is not as hard as one might think; as with most things, doing it properly (and repeating it enough) will yield good results.
• It works because it involves you — the therapist/ life coach — as a human being much more than in other kinds of therapy. During the initial stages of the therapy, you will be responsible for helping the person in question, and you simply need to be there, even if not planned. I already explained this before. The "separation method" will not only change how your client feels about him/herself, the past, the present, or the future; I hope it will also change the way *you* feel about yourself (as a therapist, life coach, counselor) and your own career. Very few things can compete with the feeling that you have helped another human being, that you have put your energy and passion into it – in

other words – you did your best, and it worked *because* of that.

Epilogue

Dear reader,

I hope you found some of the content of this book useful. I hope you learned something, confirmed something, or questioned something! After all, that is why we are here, on this Earth – to question, learn, improve, and help. If, after reading this book, you feel inspired to help another human being you know (yourself included) in any way, then this book has done what it was meant to do.

If you agree or disagree with what you have read in this book, feel free to start a discussion; that is one of the ways we learn – by exchanging ideas.

Lastly, I wish to express my gratitude for being alive and well, for having my family and friends, and for being able to share my thoughts and help another human being.

Indeed, what more could one ask for?

ABOUT THE AUTHOR

Maja Spencer (Serbian: Maja Spenser) was born in 1983 in Yugoslavia. She graduated from the University of Political Sciences, Department of International Relations, in 2005. First, she was in love with the fields of security, propaganda, and manipulation. After many years of studying psychology, sociology, and psychopathology, she started writing books. She also holds a Master's degree in psychology.

Spencer has authored "Needless Thinking about Needs", "Humanoid", "Something Is Wrong", "Beside Yourself, Around Yourself, and Back to Yourself", "The Empathy Switch", "Simple State of Happiness", and "In The Trap of Cognitive Dissonance".

She has composed and performed music for her four albums and numerous singles.

When she gets the chance, Maja likes to dance Argentinian tango; she also enjoys shooting firearms, running, free dancing, drawing, interior design, reading, and driving.

Maja is a mother, daughter, sister, friend, and a source of support for anyone in need. She is not a member of any political, religious, or other group or association.

INDEPENDENT MEDIA, SLU

2023

www.ingramcontent.com/pod-product-compliance
Lightning Source LLC
Chambersburg PA
CBHW031314250726
48656CB00005B/1787